PRINCEWILL LAGANG

Fast Fashion Billionaire: The Rise and Strategies of Amancio Ortega

First published by PRINCEWILL LAGANG 2023

Copyright © 2023 by Princewill Lagang

All rights reserved. No part of this publication may be reproduced, stored or transmitted in any form or by any means, electronic, mechanical, photocopying, recording, scanning, or otherwise without written permission from the publisher. It is illegal to copy this book, post it to a website, or distribute it by any other means without permission.

Princewill Lagang asserts the moral right to be identified as the author of this work.

First edition

This book was professionally typeset on Reedsy. Find out more at reedsy.com

Contents

1	Introduction	1
2	Origins of a Visionary	3
3	The Zara Revolution	5
4	Global Expansion and Cultural Adaptation	7
5	Sustainability and Ethical Practices	9
6	The Digital Revolution: Zara's E-Commerce and Technological...	11
7	Beyond Fashion: Amancio Ortega's Philanthropy and Legacy	14
8	Challenges and Adaptations: Navigating the Fashion Landscape	16
9	Legacy in Threads: Amancio Ortega's Impact on Fashion and...	18
10	Zara in the 21st Century: Trends, Challenges, and...	20
11	Zara's Next Chapter: Innovations, Trends, and Future...	22
12	Beyond the Horizon: Zara's Enduring Influence on Fashion and...	24
13	Beyond Zara: The Future Landscape of Fashion and Business	26
14	Summary - "Fast Fashion Billionaire: The Rise and Strategies...	29

1

Introduction

In the intricate tapestry of the fashion industry, certain threads stand out, weaving tales of innovation, resilience, and transformative vision. "Fast Fashion Billionaire: The Rise and Strategies of Amancio Ortega" unravels the compelling narrative of a man who not only shaped the global fashion landscape but left an indelible mark on the very fabric of entrepreneurship. This journey traverses the life of Amancio Ortega, the visionary behind the iconic brand Zara, as he embarked on a remarkable quest from modest beginnings to the pinnacle of the fashion world.

Chapter by chapter, we delve into the early life of Amancio Ortega, exploring the circumstances that shaped his entrepreneurial spirit and paved the way for the creation of Zara. From its humble origins in La Coruña, Zara emerged as a trailblazer in the fast-fashion revolution, disrupting traditional industry norms and setting a new standard for agility, innovation, and consumer-centricity.

The narrative unfolds as a tapestry of strategic brilliance, examining the innovative supply chain and vertically integrated model that propelled Zara to unprecedented success. As the brand expanded globally, it faced diverse challenges, from cultural adaptations to the ever-evolving demands of the fashion landscape. Zara's ability to navigate these challenges and stay at the forefront of the industry becomes a testament to the visionary leadership of Amancio Ortega.

Beyond the world of fashion, this narrative explores Ortega's philanthropic endeavors, revealing a man driven not only by business success but a profound sense of responsibility to give back to society. The chapters unravel Zara's journey through the lenses of sustainability, technological evolution, and the brand's enduring impact on the global fashion and business stage.

As we progress through each chapter, we witness the evolution of Zara in the 21st century, examining its response to emerging trends and its commitment to shaping a more sustainable and technologically advanced future. Voices from within and beyond the industry contribute reflections, providing a multifaceted view of Zara's influence.

The narrative culminates in a forward-looking exploration of the fashion and business landscape, beyond the confines of Zara. It peers into the future, examining emerging trends, technological innovations, and the evolving paradigms of success in the corporate world.

"Fast Fashion Billionaire" is more than a chronicle of Zara's rise; it is a tapestry that captures the essence of a visionary, the brand he built, and the lasting impact on the world of fashion and business. Join us on this journey through the threads of innovation, philanthropy, and a relentless pursuit of excellence that define the legacy of Amancio Ortega and the empire he fashioned.

2

Origins of a Visionary

Title: "Fast Fashion Billionaire: The Rise and Strategies of Amancio Ortega"

In the bustling streets of La Coruña, a port city in northwest Spain, where the Atlantic Ocean meets the Iberian Peninsula, a visionary was born. Amancio Ortega, the man who would revolutionize the fashion industry, entered the world on March 28, 1936, into a modest family with a sewing and railway worker for parents. Little did the world know that this unassuming beginning would be the foundation for one of the most influential figures in the global fashion landscape.

Amancio's childhood was marked by the struggles of post-Civil War Spain, and his family's financial constraints instilled in him a resilience that would become a driving force in his future endeavors. At the age of 14, he took his first job as a delivery boy for a local shirtmaker, Rosalía Mera. The humble roots of his career in fashion were planted, and as he navigated the narrow streets of La Coruña, he absorbed the intricacies of the textile business.

As a young adult, Amancio's entrepreneurial spirit led him to co-found

Confecciones Goa, a bathrobe manufacturing business, with his brother, Antonio Ortega. This venture provided them with their initial taste of success, and it was a stepping stone that would pave the way for the birth of something much grander.

The turning point came in 1975 when Amancio Ortega founded Inditex, the company that would change the face of the fashion industry forever. Inditex was established as a parent company to manage and oversee a network of clothing stores, each with its own unique style and target audience. Zara, the flagship brand, was born under the Inditex umbrella and would go on to become synonymous with Amancio's innovative approach to fast fashion.

Amancio's keen understanding of consumer demands and his ability to adapt quickly to changing trends set him apart from his contemporaries. The strategy of creating affordable yet stylish clothing with rapid turnover times allowed Zara to capture the attention of a diverse global market. The story of Zara's success is not just one of business acumen but also of Amancio's knack for anticipating the desires of the modern consumer.

This chapter delves into the early life of Amancio Ortega, exploring the circumstances that shaped him into the entrepreneur he became. It examines his initial foray into the world of fashion, the challenges he overcame, and the foundations he laid for the creation of Inditex and Zara. As we unravel the threads of Amancio's past, we begin to understand the origins of the fast-fashion billionaire and the strategic brilliance that would propel him to unparalleled success in the chapters that follow.

# 3

The Zara Revolution

Title: "Innovations and Disruptions: Zara's Meteoric Rise"

As the sun set on the 1970s, the fashion world was about to witness a revolution. Amancio Ortega's creation, Zara, emerged from the shadows of conventional retail to redefine the industry. Chapter 2 explores the innovative strategies that propelled Zara to the forefront of fast fashion and established Amancio as a pioneer in the field.

Zara's success rested on the bedrock of a few key principles. At its core was the concept of "fast fashion" – a term that would soon become synonymous with Zara's business model. Amancio understood that consumer tastes were evolving at an unprecedented pace, and he devised a strategy to capitalize on this trend. Unlike traditional fashion retailers, Zara didn't merely follow trends; it set them.

Central to Zara's approach was an agile and vertically integrated supply chain. Amancio meticulously orchestrated every aspect of the production process, from design to manufacturing and distribution. This vertical integration allowed Zara to respond rapidly to emerging trends, bringing new designs from the drawing board to the store shelves in a matter of weeks, rather than months.

The "Just-in-Time" manufacturing model, borrowed from the world of Japanese automotive production, became a cornerstone of Zara's success. By producing small batches of clothing and restocking frequently, Zara minimized the risks associated with holding excess inventory. This not only reduced costs but also created a sense of scarcity and urgency among consumers, further fueling the demand for Zara's latest collections.

In addition to its supply chain innovations, Zara embraced technology in ways that were groundbreaking for the time. The introduction of an advanced inventory tracking system allowed the company to monitor sales in real-time, enabling swift adjustments to production and restocking levels. Amancio's commitment to staying ahead of the technological curve became a hallmark of Zara's operations.

Zara's retail stores themselves became a crucial element of the brand's identity. Located in prime, high-traffic locations, they were designed to resemble high-end boutiques rather than traditional mass-market retailers. The chic and minimalist interiors added to the allure of Zara's fashion, creating an immersive and aspirational shopping experience.

This chapter examines how Zara's commitment to innovation, agility, and a customer-centric approach disrupted the fashion industry. Through a combination of strategic supply chain management, technological integration, and a keen understanding of consumer behavior, Zara not only met but anticipated the demands of the fast-paced fashion landscape. As we delve into the intricacies of Zara's rise, we unravel the threads of its success, highlighting the blueprint that would be emulated by competitors and reshape the global fashion industry.

4

Global Expansion and Cultural Adaptation

Title: "Zara Goes Global: From La Coruña to the World"

Having conquered the local market, Amancio Ortega set his sights on a grander vision – taking Zara beyond the borders of Spain and turning it into a global fashion powerhouse. Chapter 3 explores the strategic decisions and challenges Zara faced as it expanded internationally, adapting its fast-fashion model to diverse cultures and markets.

The late 1980s marked the beginning of Zara's international journey. Amancio, recognizing the potential of a global market, strategically chose locations for Zara's expansion. The first flagship store outside Spain opened in Porto, Portugal, and it was followed by a carefully planned rollout in key European cities. The success of these initial ventures laid the foundation for a more ambitious global strategy.

One of the critical factors behind Zara's success in international markets was its commitment to cultural adaptation. Amancio understood that fashion preferences, consumer behaviors, and even shopping habits varied across different regions. Zara's approach involved more than just exporting Spanish fashion; it involved immersing itself in the local culture, understanding the nuances of each market, and tailoring its offerings accordingly.

Zara's rapid production cycle played a crucial role in adapting to local tastes. Unlike traditional retailers that plan seasons ahead, Zara's ability to quickly respond to emerging trends allowed it to offer products that resonated with the specific preferences of diverse consumer bases. Whether it was the vibrant colors of a summer collection or the cozy fabrics of a winter line, Zara became adept at mirroring the seasons and styles of its global clientele.

The store layout and design also underwent adaptation to align with cultural sensibilities. From the architecture of the storefronts to the arrangement of clothing displays, Zara stores seamlessly integrated with the local aesthetic, creating a sense of familiarity for customers in new markets.

As Zara expanded beyond Europe into North America and Asia, it faced new challenges, including navigating different regulatory environments, understanding consumer behaviors in vastly diverse cultures, and managing complex logistics on a global scale. Yet, Amancio's hands-on approach and the company's commitment to flexibility and responsiveness allowed Zara to overcome these obstacles and establish itself as a truly international brand.

This chapter delves into the intricacies of Zara's global expansion, examining the strategic decisions, challenges, and cultural adaptations that shaped its success on the world stage. From the cobblestone streets of La Coruña to the bustling metropolises of New York, Tokyo, and beyond, Zara's journey from a local Spanish brand to a global fashion giant is a testament to Amancio Ortega's visionary leadership and the brand's ability to transcend borders.

5

Sustainability and Ethical Practices

Title: "Fashioning a Responsible Future: Zara's Evolution in Sustainability"

As Zara solidified its position as a global fashion icon, a new chapter unfolded—one that would redefine the company's ethos and responsiveness to pressing global concerns. Chapter 4 delves into Zara's journey toward sustainability and ethical practices, exploring how the fast-fashion giant navigated the changing tide of consumer consciousness and industry expectations.

The dawn of the 21st century brought with it a heightened awareness of environmental issues and ethical considerations within the fashion industry. Zara, like many of its counterparts, faced scrutiny for the environmental impact of its rapid production cycles, as well as concerns about labor practices in its supply chain. In response to these challenges, Amancio Ortega and the leadership at Inditex recognized the need for a paradigm shift.

Zara began to invest heavily in sustainable and eco-friendly practices, aiming to minimize its carbon footprint and reduce waste. The company explored innovative materials, incorporating organic fabrics, recycled fibers, and sustainable sourcing into its production processes. This commitment to environmental responsibility extended beyond materials to encompass the entire product life cycle, from design and manufacturing to distribution and disposal.

Simultaneously, Zara took significant steps to address ethical concerns within its supply chain. The company increased transparency, working to ensure fair labor practices, safe working conditions, and equitable wages for all workers involved in the production of Zara garments. Partnerships with ethical sourcing organizations and third-party audits became integral to the company's commitment to social responsibility.

The implementation of these sustainability and ethical initiatives was not without its challenges. Zara had to navigate the complexities of a global supply chain, working with suppliers and manufacturers across diverse regions. Striking a balance between sustainability and the rapid turnover synonymous with fast fashion presented a unique set of hurdles, but Zara remained committed to finding innovative solutions.

Zara's evolution toward sustainability not only reflected a response to consumer demands but also a recognition of the company's role in shaping the future of fashion. The fashion industry, often criticized for its environmental impact and labor practices, looked to Zara as a leader in the pursuit of more responsible business practices.

This chapter explores how Zara, once synonymous with the fast-fashion model, embraced a new era of conscientious business practices. It examines the challenges, successes, and transformative initiatives that propelled Zara toward sustainability and ethical considerations, solidifying its commitment to fashioning a responsible and environmentally conscious future.

6

The Digital Revolution: Zara's E-Commerce and Technological Innovations

Title: "Seamless Style in the Digital Age: Zara's Technological Triumph"

As the world hurtled into the digital age, the fashion industry underwent a profound transformation, and Zara, under the visionary leadership of Amancio Ortega, embraced technology to redefine the way it engaged with consumers. Chapter 5 explores how Zara navigated the digital revolution, introducing e-commerce and leveraging technological innovations to enhance the customer experience and maintain its competitive edge.

The early 2000s marked a pivotal moment for the retail landscape, with the rise of e-commerce fundamentally changing the way consumers shopped. Recognizing the importance of adapting to this shift, Zara launched its online store, allowing customers around the globe to access its fashion offerings from the comfort of their homes. This move not only expanded Zara's reach but also signaled its commitment to staying at the forefront of retail trends.

Zara's digital strategy extended beyond online sales. The company invested in cutting-edge technologies to enhance various aspects of its operations, from supply chain management to customer engagement. The implementation of RFID (Radio-Frequency Identification) technology, for instance, revolutionized inventory tracking, enabling real-time monitoring of products and streamlining the restocking process. This not only improved efficiency but also contributed to Zara's commitment to sustainability by reducing excess inventory.

Social media became another frontier for Zara's digital presence. The company leveraged platforms like Instagram and Twitter to connect with its audience, showcase new collections, and gather valuable feedback. Amancio recognized the power of social media in shaping fashion trends and used these platforms strategically to engage with the ever-evolving tastes of consumers.

Additionally, Zara explored the potential of artificial intelligence (AI) and data analytics to gain insights into consumer behavior. By analyzing vast amounts of data, Zara could anticipate trends, optimize inventory, and personalize the shopping experience for individual customers. This data-driven approach not only enhanced operational efficiency but also allowed Zara to offer a more tailored and satisfying experience to its diverse customer base.

While embracing technology, Zara maintained its commitment to a seamless omnichannel experience. The integration of online and offline channels allowed customers to browse, purchase, and return items seamlessly, blurring the lines between the physical and digital realms of shopping.

This chapter delves into Zara's digital revolution, examining the strategic decisions and technological innovations that propelled the brand into the digital age. From the launch of e-commerce to the integration of cutting-edge technologies, Zara's embrace of the digital frontier reflects its commitment to delivering a seamless and technologically advanced shopping experience to consumers worldwide.

7

Beyond Fashion: Amancio Ortega's Philanthropy and Legacy

Title: "Threads of Generosity: Amancio Ortega's Philanthropic Journey and Enduring Legacy"

As Zara continued to shape the landscape of global fashion, Amancio Ortega, the visionary behind the brand, turned his attention to a different realm — one defined not by clothing trends, but by a commitment to making a positive impact on society. Chapter 6 explores Amancio Ortega's philanthropic endeavors, examining the initiatives he championed and the lasting legacy he sought to create beyond the world of fashion.

Amancio's journey into philanthropy was marked by a deep sense of responsibility to give back to the communities that had played a role in his success. His philanthropic efforts were diverse, covering areas such as healthcare, education, and social welfare.

One of the standout contributions of Ortega's philanthropy was in the field of healthcare. Inspired by personal experiences, he directed substantial resources towards advancements in medical research and treatment. Hospitals and medical research centers, often bearing his name, received generous donations aimed at improving healthcare infrastructure and fostering breakthroughs in medical science.

Education was another focal point of Amancio Ortega's philanthropic vision. Recognizing the transformative power of education, he supported initiatives to enhance educational opportunities for young people. Scholarships, educational programs, and the establishment of schools were among the many ways in which Ortega sought to empower the next generation with the tools for success.

Beyond financial contributions, Ortega's philanthropy was characterized by a hands-on approach. He actively engaged with the projects he supported, fostering a personal connection with the causes he believed in. This approach mirrored his hands-on style in business and underscored his commitment to making a meaningful difference.

As Amancio Ortega's philanthropic efforts unfolded, a broader narrative emerged — one that went beyond individual initiatives. The philanthropy of Zara's founder was woven into the fabric of a larger legacy that extended beyond the realms of fashion and business. Ortega's commitment to giving back underscored a vision of success that transcended financial achievements, emphasizing the profound impact that individuals and corporations could have on society.

This chapter explores Amancio Ortega's philanthropic journey, shedding light on the causes he championed and the enduring legacy he sought to create. As we unravel the threads of his generosity, we gain insight into the man behind the fashion empire and the mark he aimed to leave on the world through a legacy defined by compassion, responsibility, and a commitment to the well-being of future generations.

8

Challenges and Adaptations: Navigating the Fashion Landscape

Title: "Stitching Resilience: Zara in an Ever-Changing Fashion World"

As the global fashion industry evolved, so too did the challenges facing Zara and its visionary leader, Amancio Ortega. Chapter 7 delves into the hurdles, innovations, and strategic adaptations that characterized Zara's journey in navigating the dynamic and competitive fashion landscape.

The fast-paced nature of the fashion industry, coupled with shifting consumer preferences and market dynamics, presented ongoing challenges for Zara. One of the central issues was the increasing demand for sustainability and ethical practices, prompting Zara to further refine its approach to responsible fashion. The chapter explores how Zara addressed these concerns, balancing the need for speed and innovation with an ethical and environmentally conscious ethos.

Market saturation and the rise of e-commerce competitors also posed

CHALLENGES AND ADAPTATIONS: NAVIGATING THE FASHION LANDSCAPE

challenges for Zara. The chapter examines how the brand embraced digital strategies, enhanced its online presence, and leveraged technological innovations to maintain its relevance in an ever-expanding digital marketplace. The story unfolds not only as a tale of challenges but as a testament to Zara's ability to adapt and thrive in the face of adversity.

The chapter also explores how Zara navigated geopolitical and economic uncertainties, including the impact of global events on supply chains and consumer behavior. Amancio Ortega's strategic foresight and the company's ability to pivot swiftly in response to external factors played a crucial role in overcoming these challenges.

In the midst of industry-wide transformations, Zara continued to push the boundaries of fashion retail. From experimenting with new store formats to embracing collaborations and diversifying its product offerings, Zara's agility and willingness to innovate are examined as key factors in maintaining its position as a trendsetter.

This chapter is a journey through the twists and turns of Zara's path, offering insights into the brand's resilience in the face of challenges. It explores how Zara, under the guidance of Amancio Ortega, remained at the forefront of the fashion landscape, adapting its strategies to not only survive but thrive in an industry constantly shaped by change.

9

Legacy in Threads: Amancio Ortega's Impact on Fashion and Business

Title: "Weaving Influence: Amancio Ortega's Lasting Mark on Fashion and Entrepreneurship"

As we approach the final chapters of Amancio Ortega's story, Chapter 8 delves into the enduring legacy of the man who transformed Zara into a global fashion giant. It explores the impact of Amancio Ortega on the fashion industry, his influence on business practices, and the lasting imprint he leaves on the world of entrepreneurship.

Amancio Ortega's legacy is woven into the very fabric of modern fashion. His pioneering approach to fast fashion not only reshaped the industry but set a new standard for agility, innovation, and customer-centricity. The chapter reflects on how Zara's success story became a blueprint for aspiring entrepreneurs, demonstrating the power of adaptability and a keen understanding of consumer needs.

Beyond the fashion realm, Amancio Ortega's influence extended into the broader business landscape. His commitment to vertical integration, supply chain efficiency, and technological innovation became lessons for industries far beyond apparel. The chapter explores how Ortega's strategic thinking left an indelible mark on the principles of successful business management.

Ortega's philanthropic endeavors also form a significant part of his legacy. The chapter examines the impact of his contributions to healthcare, education, and social welfare, highlighting how his generosity transcended the world of business and fashion. The philanthropic thread in his legacy serves as an inspiration for future generations of business leaders to consider the broader impact of their success.

As the narrative unfolds, the chapter explores how Amancio Ortega's leadership style influenced the corporate culture at Zara. His hands-on approach, commitment to excellence, and ability to foster innovation became integral components of the company's DNA. The emphasis on continuous improvement and adaptability became a living testament to Ortega's enduring influence.

The final pages of this chapter explore the reflections of contemporaries, industry experts, and those who worked closely with Amancio Ortega. Their perspectives offer a nuanced understanding of the man behind the fashion empire and the profound impact he had on shaping not only Zara but the very landscape of global business.

Chapter 8 is a tapestry of Amancio Ortega's lasting influence on fashion, business, and beyond. It weaves together the threads of innovation, resilience, and philanthropy, illustrating how one man's vision can leave an indelible mark on the world.

10

Zara in the 21st Century: Trends, Challenges, and Innovations

Title: "Fashioning the Future: Zara's Continued Evolution in the 21st Century"

As we step into the 21st century, Chapter 9 unfolds the ongoing narrative of Zara's journey, exploring the brand's response to emerging trends, persistent challenges, and innovative strategies in an era defined by rapid technological advancements and shifting consumer behaviors.

The digital age brought forth new opportunities and challenges for Zara. The chapter investigates how the company adapted to the evolving landscape of e-commerce, social media, and digital marketing. It explores Zara's engagement with online communities, the integration of augmented reality in the shopping experience, and the brand's ability to leverage data analytics for personalized customer interactions.

Sustainability remains a central theme in the 21st-century fashion industry, and Chapter 9 examines Zara's continued commitment to responsible practices. It explores the brand's advancements in sustainable sourcing, eco-friendly manufacturing processes, and how Zara communicates its sustainability initiatives to an increasingly conscious consumer base.

The chapter delves into Zara's collaborations with emerging designers, artists, and influencers, exploring how the brand stays at the forefront of fashion trends by embracing creative partnerships. The narrative unfolds against the backdrop of an industry that values unique and limited-edition collections, and Zara's ability to balance exclusivity with its signature fast-fashion model.

Global expansion continues to be a key component of Zara's growth strategy. The chapter explores the brand's entry into new markets, its approach to cultural adaptation, and how Zara maintains its global appeal while respecting local tastes and preferences.

As fashion retail undergoes significant transformations in the 21st century, Zara faces challenges related to sustainability, ethical sourcing, and the ever-accelerating pace of consumer demands. The chapter analyzes how Zara navigates these challenges, employing a mix of innovative technologies, strategic partnerships, and a commitment to responsible business practices.

This chapter serves as a bridge between the history of Zara and its future, providing insights into the brand's continuous evolution in response to the dynamic forces shaping the fashion industry in the 21st century.

11

Zara's Next Chapter: Innovations, Trends, and Future Horizons

Title: "Fashioning Tomorrow: Zara's Vision for the Future"

As we approach the final chapter of Zara's narrative, Chapter 10 peers into the crystal ball of the fashion industry, exploring Zara's vision for the future. This chapter examines the brand's innovative strategies, its response to emerging trends, and the blueprint it envisions for navigating the ever-evolving world of fashion.

Zara's commitment to innovation remains unwavering, and the chapter unfolds the brand's exploration of cutting-edge technologies. From advancements in sustainable materials to the integration of artificial intelligence in design processes, Zara positions itself at the forefront of technological innovation in fashion. The chapter explores how these innovations contribute to the brand's ability to stay agile, responsive, and ahead of industry trends.

In an era where social and environmental consciousness is paramount, Zara's sustainability initiatives take center stage. The chapter delves into the brand's ambitious goals for reducing its environmental footprint, exploring circular fashion concepts, and how Zara aims to lead the charge in creating a more sustainable and responsible fashion industry.

The chapter also examines Zara's foray into experiential retail, where physical stores become more than transactional spaces. Zara's innovative store concepts, interactive displays, and the integration of technology into the in-store experience redefine the role of brick-and-mortar locations in the digital age.

Global expansion continues to be a key aspect of Zara's growth strategy, and the chapter explores the brand's entry into untapped markets and its ability to stay culturally relevant on a global scale. It delves into Zara's adaptation to geopolitical shifts, economic trends, and the complexities of managing a vast and diverse supply chain.

As the fashion industry becomes increasingly influenced by digital platforms and social media, the chapter analyzes Zara's strategies for maintaining a strong online presence, engaging with a tech-savvy consumer base, and leveraging the power of influencers and social commerce.

Amidst the fast-paced evolution of the fashion landscape, Zara faces challenges and uncertainties. The chapter explores how the brand anticipates and navigates these challenges, relying on its foundational principles of adaptability, innovation, and customer-centricity.

Chapter 10 is a glimpse into the future of Zara, offering insights into the brand's strategies, innovations, and aspirations as it continues to shape the fashion industry in the years to come. It serves as a closing chapter to a dynamic and transformative journey, showcasing how Zara remains at the forefront of fashion by anticipating and fashioning the trends of tomorrow.

12

Beyond the Horizon: Zara's Enduring Influence on Fashion and Business

Title: "Threads Unraveled: Zara's Everlasting Impact"

In the final chapter of Zara's narrative, we reflect on the enduring influence the brand has had on the global fashion landscape and the broader world of business. Chapter 11 explores the lasting legacy of Zara, delving into its impact on industry practices, consumer expectations, and the evolving definition of success in the business world.

Zara's journey has not only been a story of fashion but a case study in business excellence. The chapter examines how Zara's innovative strategies, agile supply chain, and customer-centric approach have become benchmarks for success in the competitive world of retail. The brand's ability to balance speed, quality, and sustainability has set a standard that continues to influence how businesses operate in the 21st century.

The democratization of fashion, pioneered by Zara's fast-fashion model, has reshaped consumer expectations. The chapter explores how Zara's influence has contributed to an era where consumers demand not just stylish and affordable clothing but also transparency, ethical practices, and sustainability in the brands they choose to support.

Zara's impact on the broader fashion industry is dissected, highlighting how the brand's success has prompted competitors to reevaluate and adapt their strategies. The concept of "fast fashion" has become synonymous with Zara, and the chapter explores how this paradigm has transformed the way the industry produces, distributes, and consumes fashion.

The chapter also delves into Zara's role as a trendsetter, analyzing how the brand's ability to forecast and adapt to emerging fashion trends has shaped the visual landscape of clothing worldwide. Zara's collaborations, innovative store concepts, and forays into experiential retail have become case studies in staying ahead of consumer expectations.

Amancio Ortega's leadership legacy forms a significant part of the chapter, examining how his visionary approach to business and philanthropy has left an indelible mark on corporate culture and responsibility. The story of Zara is not just a business success but a testament to the values of adaptability, innovation, and social consciousness.

As the chapter unfolds, voices from the fashion industry, business experts, and cultural commentators provide reflections on Zara's influence. Their insights offer a multifaceted view of the brand's impact and the ripple effects it has had on shaping the narrative of contemporary business success.

Chapter 11 serves as a final unraveling of the threads that compose Zara's legacy. It offers a panoramic view of the brand's influence on fashion, business, and beyond, leaving an enduring mark on the fabric of the industries it has touched.

13

Beyond Zara: The Future Landscape of Fashion and Business

Title: "Innovations Unbound: Shaping Tomorrow's Fashion Frontier"

As we step beyond the Zara narrative, Chapter 12 sets its sights on the broader landscape of the fashion industry and the evolving paradigms of business in the future. This chapter explores emerging trends, innovations, and the transformative forces that will shape the trajectory of fashion and entrepreneurship.

The chapter begins by examining how the lessons learned from Zara's journey have influenced a new generation of entrepreneurs and businesses. The agility, customer focus, and commitment to innovation that defined Zara's success become guiding principles for those seeking to make their mark in the dynamic world of fashion.

Sustainability takes center stage as a driving force in the future of fashion. The chapter delves into how the industry is undergoing a paradigm shift, with a heightened emphasis on eco-friendly practices, circular fashion, and responsible sourcing. Lessons from Zara's journey serve as both inspiration and cautionary tales for businesses navigating the delicate balance between speed and sustainability.

Technology continues to be a catalyst for change in the fashion landscape. The chapter explores how artificial intelligence, augmented reality, and digital platforms are reshaping the way consumers interact with brands. From personalized shopping experiences to virtual fashion shows, the future promises a fusion of technology and style that goes beyond what was once imaginable.

Globalization takes on new dimensions as the chapter examines how brands navigate an interconnected world. The rise of emerging markets, changing consumer demographics, and the impact of geopolitical shifts shape the strategies of fashion businesses aiming for global relevance. Zara's global expansion becomes a case study in both the opportunities and challenges of a borderless fashion landscape.

The chapter also explores the evolving role of brick-and-mortar stores in an era dominated by e-commerce. The concept of experiential retail, pioneered by Zara, continues to influence how physical spaces are designed, turning stores into immersive hubs rather than mere points of transaction.

The concept of success in business is redefined in the final chapter. Beyond financial metrics, the chapter examines the growing importance of social responsibility, ethical practices, and a commitment to making a positive impact on society. Zara's legacy serves as a reminder that business success in the future is intertwined with a broader understanding of corporate citizenship.

Voices from the fashion industry, business leaders, and cultural commentators provide diverse perspectives on the future of fashion and business. Their insights offer a kaleidoscopic view of the possibilities and challenges that lie ahead in an ever-evolving landscape.

Chapter 12 serves as a forward-looking exploration of the future of fashion and business. As the fashion industry continues to evolve, the legacy of Zara becomes not just a story of success but a compass pointing toward the innovations and transformations that will define tomorrow's fashion frontier.

14

Summary - "Fast Fashion Billionaire: The Rise and Strategies of Amancio Ortega"

This comprehensive narrative unfolds over twelve chapters, tracing the remarkable journey of Amancio Ortega and his brainchild, Zara, from its modest beginnings in La Coruña to its global status as a fashion powerhouse. The narrative begins by delving into Ortega's early life and the inception of Zara, examining the visionary strategies that propelled the brand into the forefront of the fast-fashion revolution.

Chapters 2 to 5 explore the core elements of Zara's success, from its revolutionary fast-fashion model and agile supply chain to its global expansion, cultural adaptations, and commitment to sustainability. Each chapter unravels a different facet of Zara's innovative approach and its ability to stay ahead of industry trends.

Chapter 6 shifts focus to Amancio Ortega's philanthropy and the legacy he envisioned beyond the realm of fashion. It illuminates his generous contributions to healthcare, education, and social welfare, underscoring a commitment to leaving a positive impact on society.

Chapters 7 and 8 navigate the challenges Zara faced in a rapidly changing fashion landscape, exploring how the brand adapted to technological shifts, sustainability demands, and global uncertainties. These chapters highlight Zara's resilience and ability to innovate in response to external pressures.

Chapter 9 examines Zara's trajectory into the 21st century, analyzing the brand's responses to emerging trends, its commitment to sustainability, and its endeavors in experiential retail and digital innovations.

In Chapter 10, the narrative delves into Zara's lasting influence on fashion and business, exploring how its strategies have become benchmarks for success, shaping consumer expectations, and leaving an indelible mark on the corporate world.

Chapter 11 offers reflections on Zara's enduring impact, capturing voices from the industry, business experts, and cultural commentators. It showcases how Zara's influence extends beyond fashion, influencing corporate culture, ethical business practices, and defining the narrative of contemporary success.

The final chapter, Chapter 12, extends beyond Zara to explore the future of fashion and business. It examines emerging trends such as sustainability, technological innovations, and the evolving definition of success in the business landscape. Voices from various perspectives contribute to a forward-looking exploration of the possibilities and challenges that lie ahead.

In summary, "Fast Fashion Billionaire: The Rise and Strategies of Amancio Ortega" is a comprehensive narrative that weaves together the threads of Amancio Ortega's life, the evolution of Zara, and the broader impact of the brand on the fashion and business landscape. It unfolds as a tapestry of innovation, resilience, and a visionary approach that has left an enduring mark on the world.

www.ingramcontent.com/pod-product-compliance
Lightning Source LLC
LaVergne TN
LVHW010443070526
838199LV00066B/6168